Cherished

Clay

A collection of poetry

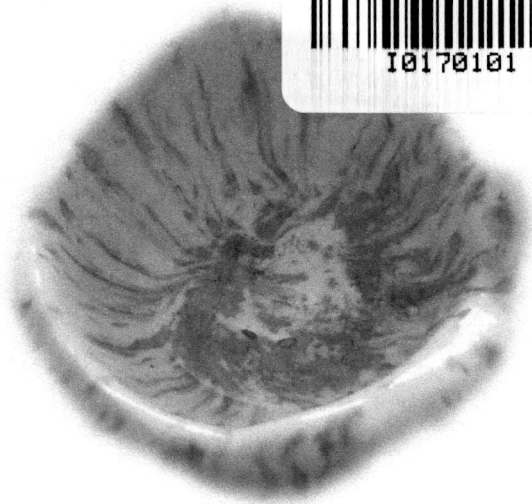

by Suzanne Searcy Johnson

1st Edition
ISBN: 978-0-9837183-3-8

suzannesjohnson.com

for Donna

Contents

1 {Now}

~

I will
Swim deeply
In the
Cleansing waters of
Now

~

Vision

In this scribbled vision
I see what could have been
And where I might have taken
My wandering heart
And I let reality fade
Behind the glimmer of fantasy

I look for a window
And find many – all locked
But it occurs to me
To shatter the glass
And make my escape
Freedom dripping down my face

It is unavoidable
This future that sends me marching
Down my chosen highway
Detours forbidden
Exits unreachable
I must go where I must

Find me here
And spread out the highway
Like a picnic blanket
And let the breeze remove
All those white dashes
And give me a blank page
To write on

Portal

I found your
Music
In my soul
It planted and
Grew there
Full and
Flowering and
Painful
And sent me
Searching

I danced with
Him
Wrapped in his
Dark arms
Bound by the
Rhythm and
Synergy
Of these
Notes of the
Past

I want to
Know
This world of
Struggle and
Striving and
Strength

Driven by
Respect
So I won't be
Separate

Art is my
Portal
Melodies and
Words and
Paintings
That take me
Deeper into this
Realm
Further into
Beauty

History breathes
Life
Into each
Moment
Informs my
Future
And leads me to
Understanding
I am forever
Changed

Haven

Find me here
Blond child of morning
Gray eyes searching
For gentle, soft
Mother's hands
Brushing tears away
With one smooth movement

Pick me up
Carry me out of the desert
Into cool summer sun
Wading in clean streams
Letting nature's feather fingers
Caress my curved shoulders
In the glow of daylight

Take me home
Not to the tired, rusted place
But to the new house of
Blessed brick and sturdy columns
Wrap me in safety
And sing to me of second chances
Here in my pure, hope-filled haven

Let Yourself Go

Let yourself go
There is pain in your soul
Heartache – caused by someone else
But you cling to it
That rope of hurt that dangles you
Over the river of contentment
You hold on 'til the burns on your
Clenched fingers bleed their sorrow
There is nothing to be gained by
Holding on to that rope
Let yourself go

Let yourself go
There is anger in your soul
You're standing somewhere between
Vulnerability and hatred
Do not lean toward loathing
The fire of anger keeps you warm for
A little while
But do not be fooled
Let it burn and it will consume your very being –
The essence of your self
And leave behind the soot and ashes of bitterness
There is nothing to be gained by
Planting your feet in anger
Let yourself go

Let yourself go
There is sadness in your soul
You mourn the loss of innocence
Like a mother crying for her stillborn baby
Looking back gives you something to touch –
Something to stir the emotions buried inside
Regret is the only safe avenue down
This dangerous road of feeling
But it is not enough
The tears fight to be released
Your heart strains to be heard
There is nothing to be gained by
Locking the door to your sadness
Let yourself go

Let yourself go
There is happiness hidden in your soul
It is afraid to peek out
So many times it has been smothered at
Its moment of emergence
You fear the newness of joy
Uncertainty traps you in false comfort
It is all you know
But it is not peace
You block the laughter that could
Soften your heart and exhilarate your very toes
There is nothing to be gained by
Sheltering yourself from happiness
Let yourself go

Now

I have
Given up on
Forever
Clinging instead to
This moment

I crave

Bliss

My child's face
Buried
In my neck

Raw sex

Words that
Move my very
Soul

Touchdowns

Burnt orange
Sunsets

Delicate harmonies

Heat

I will
Feel these
Fiercely
In my
Gut

No thought for
Outcomes
No reaching for
Elusive
Foundations

Instead I will
Swim deeply
In the
Cleansing waters of
Now

Moment

At this very moment
There is a family
Standing in a hospital waiting room
Too nervous to sit
Too scared to leave
Unsure of every step
As they pace
And wait
To hear whether she will live or die

At this very moment
There is a couple
Whose naked bodies are entwined
In rapturous lovemaking
Their minds and bodies
Are absorbed with each other
And the kisses
And the touches
Belong to the joining of their existence

At this very moment
There is a man
Sitting on a street corner
Sign held by his beggar's hands
His mind cannot hold a thought
And fear has become his soulmate
And he waits
And hopes
For enough coins to sustain him through the
night

At this very moment
There is a baby
Fighting her way through her mother's womb
Moving to find what awaits outside
And her mind cannot know
And her heart cannot sense
The comfort
And love
That will beckon from her mother's eyes

At this very moment
There is a man
Whose body is weakened
Who suffers constant pain
And he is ready to reach the end
Or beginning
And he prays
And he looks
To find the passage to another life

At this very moment
There is excruciating pain
And unspeakable joy
Cruelty and compassion
There is love with no boundaries
And hatred that rolls in like fog
And we are all a part of it
And it is in our bones
And this sharing of humanity –
This is life

Music

Play your sweet melodies
Sing your spirit
To the open land
Beg the sky to answer
Call the thunder
Out of its hidden place

Your music is your message
The sum of your life
Praying to be heard
And answered with a teardrop
Falling from the colorless clouds
To rest on your golden arm

Tell the story of you
Woven in these lofty notes
Let them hear you
From the green mountaintops
To the flowing, satin streams
And wait for their response

When the song returns to you
On wings of raindrop fugues
Your spirit will know truth
Your voice will echo trust
And the music will take you
To the resting place that is your destiny

Youth

You splash on
The subtle scent of youth
Gone out to play
You bathe in perfume
Of futures held
Within your fragile fingers

The world is here
Patiently tapping at
Your front door
While you sneak out the back
And tiptoe behind it
So you can own it yourself

You put the lilies
In your curls
Daisies on your wrist
And dance barefoot
Over shiny pebbles
That giggle under your feet

What a life you've given yourself
The joy of choosing
The peace of knowing
Nature's plan
You breathe in
The subtle scent of youth
That's found its home

Answer

Your answer is here
In the glass green vase
Chipped on the corner
Blood dripping from your finger
Cut on its sharp edge

Your answer is here
Pale in the moonlight
Frantic for shadows
To hide the truth
Found in these foggy beams

Your answer is here
Tasting of molasses
Slowly pouring down
The branches that give you shade
And sweet, cool breezes

Your answer is here
In my gentle hands
Gliding across your bruised back
Reaching for sensation
That awakens my sleeping soul

Your answer is here
Spiraling down the staircase
Finding splinters in your heels
Leading you to wooden statues
And accolades to cheer your arrival

Your answer is here
Screaming through the baby's cry
Pleading mother to hear
And hold you in her bosom
Of safety and forgiveness

Your answer is here
In brick and mortar
And sturdy frames
And the home you deserted
To find your grand destiny

Your answer is here
Right where you left it
In the flame of this familiar candle
Held by your lover's hands
Carrying you back
Calling you home

Loved

It was there
A warm, welcoming voice
Both in her and around her
The words – "You are loved"
Never had she felt it
Never had she known it
Truly, deeply
In her whole self –
Not just her mind

Finally, no resisting
Just tears
Washing away the wrongs
Cleansing, healing, moving
Her to newness
"You are loved"
In spite of all
In place of all
Just as she was
And all she would become

The words gave her freedom
Unlocked the doors
Flung them open
And sent her – laughing –
Out into this bright world
Never to be alone again

2 {Injustice}

~

Love is not
Silence
I must find
Courage

~

Fractured

Fractured
One nation
Divisible
Hatred and
Anger and
Strife
I am tired of
Being hostile
But kindness
Brought no
Change

Is it more
Caring to
Challenge?
Or do I
Surrender to
Inequity?
Love is not
Silence
I must find
Courage

But the
Gauntlet is
First
Thrown to me
Self-examination
Leaves me
Raw
I have been
Part of the
Problem

Lay my soul
Bare
Tell the
Stories of my
Youth
Ugly tales of
When color
Mattered to
Me
I am
Ashamed

There are those
Who are
Abandoned
I will join
My new-found
Voice with
Theirs
So the sound
Will shake the
Earth and
Cause an
Avalanche

We are
Fractured
But my
Hope is
Steadfast
If I have to
Struggle
I will
With one goal
In mind
Justice for
All

Sandy Hook

Somewhere
There is a
Child
Who saw
Blood and
Death
When he
Should have seen
Miracles

Hopes
And the
Elf on the
Shelf
Melt in this
Reality
How do we
Tell him
Santa will bring
Toys
When friends are
Gone
Forever

Love
Must cover us
All
Remind us
Tomorrow
Waits even
When we
Mourn
We hold those
Innocent
Precious
Hearts in our
Hands

We have one
Hope
They are
Strong
Resilient
And we will
Hug them
Tighter on this
Night

Control

I am in control
And I suck my strength
From the weakness of others
And I dominate

And in my power I am helpless
I command all around me
And manipulate each one
As a marionette on a string

But there is nothing holding me together
It is not that my shell is cracked
And my insides spill onto the floor

I have simply never had a covering
And I have never had an anchor to
Hold me to something
And make sense of my world

So I have chosen this path
I hold a gun in my hand
And cruelty in my bloodshot eyes
And I tell you to crawl on the floor
And you do
Because I am in control

And sooner or later
My method of control
Will land me in jail
Or get me shot
Or send me running away until I disappear
From myself
And I will be as lost as I feel in the mornings
When I awake and – for one long minute –
I can't remember my name

Color

I heard the ugliness
Couldn't believe the words
Of judgment
Venom, superiority
How can this be?

That the outward
Defines the inward
Appearance rules and
Reality is lost

But I see the
Beautiful
Richness in skin tone
Glory in diversity

And I weep –
Not for those unseen –
But for those
Mired in contempt

How lonely it must be
For them
And how sad when
They one day see
They spat on
God's magnificent treasure

Whip

Circus tent
Ringmaster's whip
Cracks on the backs of animals
Fighting fear
Rage builds

Family home
Mother's whip
Cracks on the backs of children
Fighting Fear
Rage builds

Child's room
Razor blade
Splits the vein of control
Fear fades
Life melts

Politician

Smiling demon
You charm donations from fools
And smother trusting children
And kill the life in your arena

Camouflaged evil
Out of your mouth flow
All the right words
And the people believe you

Hidden darkness
You make them dance around you
Struggling for power you wait
And prey on the weak
And cut the legs of the strong
You take what you want
And leave conscience in the closet

Smiling demon
A thin plastic veil
Is all that covers your true self
And hides your dark manipulation
But I can see your eyes

911

It hit her
That moment of knowing
Lives were being lost
Last breaths
Letting go

Their fight was over
Buried in the rubble
No rescue
Some would remain
And she cried for them

Strangers
Yet brothers, sisters
Lost in a war
Unknown to all of us
Until that day

She had to sing
To pray the word
To carry their souls
From this world
To a place of peace

And in those minutes
She was with them
Holding them in
Her heart
And the tears fell again

Way

And this is the way you own woman
And you fight your fear of her
She is strong
And stand over her with bloody fists
Because you must be stronger

And this is how you control
The person she is free to be outside this room
And you must hold her back
And force her into kitchens and stereotypes
Because she may be better than you
Or stronger inside or smarter

But you have fists
And you keep her from wearing her sexuality
Outside this room
You can keep her from seeing herself
As she is

And this is how you have power
And this is the way you beat her down
And keep her under your thumb
And you wipe the blood from your fists
With a pink hand towel
And tell her to wash it clean and crisp
And she does

Down

He is a
Buffoon
Perched on a
Throne of
Cardboard
Boxes
Fortified only with
Hate
Revered by
Angry boys with
Guns but no
Heart

Grabs what he
Wants
No thought for
Her
She is
Nothing to
Him but a
Vessel for his
Perversion
But she is
Real to
Me

Words
Even more
Ridiculous than the
Previous
Proclaimed with a
Shrug
Yet believed by
Blindfolded
Fools
Mouths open to
Receive filthy
Lies

Ugly is
More than skin
Deep
He bullies those
Who are
Beautifully
Darker than he
But glorifies the
Hideous
Soul
Reflected in the
Mirror

He ridicules the
Broken
Revels in their
Struggles and
Scoffs at
Kindness
With his
Repugnant
Snicker
Fear and
Loathing are his
Weapons

And make no
Mistake
This is brutal
War
But his
Malice and
Evil will not
Win
There is one
Certainty
He is going
Down

3 {Loss}

~

It still
Hurts
And I am left
Wondering
How I got to
This place
And where my
New self
Will reside

~

Gone

There was a smile in your eyes
I saw it before you fell into dark waters
Wonder why you chose to leave this place
For the unknown

Did you see a vision
Of clear, bright oceans pulling you
To freedom and joy?

Or was it just that time?
Didn't want to wear out your welcome
On this lonely earth

I miss your poet's heart
And the winged music that
Flew from your soul
To dance around the lucky few

My cries must be heard
Somewhere in that other realm
You must feel my presence
And know someone here
Still thinks of you
When the rains fall slowly
On autumn leaves

Heartbeat

No heartbeat
The monitor screamed at her with
Deafening silence
No heartbeat
She had seen it
Weeks before
A beautiful, beating light
A surprise blessing
A miracle given by God
Then taken away by God
Illogical
Unthinkable
There must be some mistake
And yet, still
No heartbeat

"It's for the best"
They would say
"There might have been something wrong"
She wouldn't have cared
Would have seen only perfection
No heartbeat
Why?

She cried and prayed
Sang and mourned
Until she found
Her God
Not one of giving or taking
But one of love and comfort
To walk with her through pain
And reach His arms of grace
To hold her
And give her
His heartbeat

Loss

Gone, torn
Ripped from the
Flesh
Or heart
Deep down

It is lost
I am lost
Wondering where
My rudder is
In the midst of
This storm

It is a
Slow decline
Not a "rip off
The bandaid"
Kind of loss
Rather a
Lingering
And painful
Letting go

The death of
Desire
Submission to
Reason and
Right

But it still
Hurts
And I am left
Wondering
How I got to
This place
And where my
New self
Will reside

It is not
Here

Regret

Hollow room
The pale light falls
On her weary face
There is no smile
No frown
No feeling
But emptiness
And a faint trace
Of regret

Sometimes it creeps
Out of its corner
And tugs at her heart
And memory
Sometimes it taunts her
With "might have beens"
And sends her mind
Into pits of turmoil
But tonight it just
Sings a melody
Soft and low
A gentle ache
A moment of memory

Like a prick on her finger
The blood of missed opportunity
Drops to the cold floor
Choices made
She sits in the chair
Frail hands gripping wooden arms
Mind pushing aside that
One sad thought

She concentrates on daisies
And hummingbirds
And fights her way
Free from the past
Escaping to find
Nothing

Reality fades in the mist
And leaves
Cruel fantasy
Where nothing can be touched
With tender fingers
No taste on full lips
No eyes sharing the soul
Where he doesn't exist at all
And she is alone
Alone in the pale light
That shines on her
Weary face

Linen

Linen layers
Cream rising
Folds of scratchy softness
Around her legs
Jutting edge catches
Silky seams and
Rips fabric asunder

She falls
The crystal tears escaping
Life screeching and grinding
And splitting her spirit
Into two pieces of
Crisp linen

Smooth no more
Tenderness gives way to
Cruel torn swatches of
Meaning and nothingness
That once were quilted
By baby-soft fingers
Into comforting blankets
That swaddled her
Fragile form

Linen layers
Cream rising
Heart forcing its head
Through prison bars
Searching for needle and
Thread spun by mystery
Aching to mend
Crying to clothe
Her pain-scarred legs with
Linen layers

Secrets

Where have you been?
What have you seen?
And why do you keep
Secrets
Hidden behind dark eyes
Whispered over coarse throat

Tell me, tell me
Make me crazy
And sad
To find the answers
And know the truth

The gap that separates us
Widens
Canyons of rock
Brown on brown
Sharp edges of clay
Pointing out the distance

And I stand here
While you stand there
And turn your back
On the wind that blows
On the dust that rises
And on me

Darkness

Fitful sleep
Darkness hovers
Stealing breath as it
Creeps along

It silences me
Closes the creaky
Wooden door
To my release

And the hinges
Are strong
Stronger than my
Swallowed tears

Once there was a window
Light shone through
Clean, clear glass
And I was happy
"Ignorance is bliss"

Now I see
Another calling
Somewhere past these
Chalky walls
And no stone path
To mark my progress
No steps taken

So I stretch the
Woolly blanket
Over my eyes
And feel the fibers
Scratch my cheek
And try to catch my breath
One last time
As the darkness
Creeps along

Miscommunication

Moment
Screams for
Answer and
Fire
I sit
Alone

There was a
Spark
Lost now
In the
Mire of
Miscommunication

And I
Can't even
Share it
For fear of
Weakness and
Contempt

You
Mattered
And now
It's gone
And I
Mourn

There is a
Hole
Where once was
Companionship
And I miss
You

4 {Love}

~

I hope it never
Ends
This feeling
The catching of my
Breath
When you come into
View

~

Love

There was once a
Moment
A planting
I felt it in my
Bones
With you was where I
Belonged

You see all of
Me
With one glance
The scars that I
Wear
And yet you choose to
Stay

I hope it never
Ends
This feeling
The catching of my
Breath
When you come into
View

We will face our
Challenges
Hand in hand
Stronger through our
Struggles
As we learn and
Grow

How are we so
Blessed
In this life
To have found each
Other
Two whole beings
Two loving hearts
Joined together as
One

Hear

You hear what I am saying
The words, the sounds
Flowing from my lips
And greeting your ear
And I wait for a response
Sitting on the footstool of anticipation
Eyes lit up like a firefly
I wait
Until the sun goes down
And all is clear

You hear what I am saying
That I love you
And you think it is
The fondness a little girl feels
For her snuggling kitten
Or the pounding heartbeat
Growing stronger when lips
First touch your weather-worn skin
But it is more

I said, "I love you"
And you heard it
But you did not listen to my heart
And now –
How will I coax this heart back out
Of cobwebbed corners
How will it pick up its scattered pieces
And who will tell it that
Love happens more than once
And if I tell it that
Will it listen?

Obsession

Kindness in a glance
Passion unrestrained
Bonds of trust
My obsession

Captivated by thoughts
Reveling in chains of desire
Freedom unwanted
My possession

Fulfillment out of reach
Needing the untouchable
Rewarded by pain
My lesson

Eyes telling truths
Heart begging deafness
Tears finding release
My obsession

Cover

Silk voice
Covers me
Teasing
Telling all

No secrets remain
Hidden fantasy
Bold
In the light of day

Tell me
Touch me
More of you
And more of us

Crowd me in
My corner
Tickle me
With words

Send me into
Dreams
Of soft caresses
And brutal passion

Leave me dry-mouthed
And aching deep inside
For one touch of your
Hand or
Tongue or
Body on fire

Silk voice
Cover me

Look

Look at me
See me
In the center of the room
In the center of the universe
Look at my eyes
Hear my voice

When you look away
You forget me
In the shadow
Of someone prettier
Or funnier
Or wiser

Look at me
I'll dance for you
Or challenge you
I'll remind you
Of who you can be
With me

When you turn away
I'm crazy
Blood rises to my cheeks
Manipulation seeps into my heart
And I'll do anything
To win you back

You look at me
And I turn away
And gaze intently
Into someone else's eyes
I grin impulsively
At your jealousy that
I feel on the back of my neck

I knew it was only a matter of time
Until you'd see me
In the center of the room
In the center of the universe

Real

I dreamed
You would
One day want
Me

More than a
Fix
Less than
Forever

But something
Real
Foolish me

Loved

I have loved with youth
Taking tentative steps on
A frozen pond
And searching for the path
Away from innocence

I have loved with abandon
Carelessly throwing my heart
To land on rocky hillsides
And reaching for the thrill
Of pure passion

I have loved with care
Begging a tentative soul
To trust my open arms
And spending quiet moments
In a gentle embrace

I have loved with understanding
My eyes opened
To mountains of rich honesty
Living for the day
Living in the moment

I have loved with trust
Knowing hands will catch me
When I fall into fear
And awakening to his
Gentle face and soothing touch

Love has been my constant friend
Nurturing me with tenderness
Sending desire through my bones
Wrapping me in warmth

Through all its stages it's brought me
Through infatuation, freedom, and inspiration
It finally set me down
In an open field of
Unconditional, overwhelming love

I have known the beauty
I have known the hunger
I have known the comfort
I have loved

Dreams

Sleep come
Feed my starving soul
With dreams
Of lips to caress
My smooth skin
Of hands to grip
My surrendering body
Of desire to fill
My aching need
If I must bear
This solitude
Let me feel his warmth
In my dreams

Found

Lost myself somewhere
Caught glimpses along the way
Close to giving up

You touched me
And sent tingling sensations
From your eyes to my spine

Making my way back
To the me I'd forgotten
Discovering hidden chambers

Whispers in my soul
Awaken me from my
Deep, dark sleep

Wish you could be here
To share in my return
To freedom and ecstasy

Wish you could be here
To kiss my yielding shoulder
And sense my release

Wish you could be here
To see the slow smile of contentment
Fall on my satisfied lips

Lost myself somewhere
But you touched me
And led the way back
To me

Torture

Torture
This need
To be a part of the dance

Music
Rolling melody
Singing feeling moaning movement

Rhythm
Drums beating
Constant pulsing heart pounding

Motion
Forceful rocking
Hands touching feet sliding

Torture
This need
To dance

Stay

Please stay
Stay with my needy soul
And tell me fairy tales
Of princesses and their
Handsome princes
And make me trust in
Happily ever after

Please stay
Keep me safe
In the shelter of your
Arms and hope and love
And carry me up the staircase
Growing in your garden
Covered with ivy

Please stay
And make a world
Out of empty promises
And say the words
I'll believe
Vows of shiny stone
Piled to form a wall
Of freedom

Please stay
And tell me you love me
And can't live without me
And need to share
The warmth of my touch
And that your rainbows
Will cover the clouds that hover
Over my frail body

Please stay
And assure me
That you won't
Make heavy tears form
In my eyes
Or sting me with
A dagger of rage
Or try to own my progress

Please stay
Kiss my tender cheek
And whisper comfort
And rose petals
And sweet soft raindrops
Into the soles of my shoes
And remind me what it means
To be innocent and trusting
And happy

Immersion

Immersion
Slip beneath the
Cooling waters

Fingers tingle
Waves fill every crevice
Every empty essence of
Meaningful existence

Ride the crest
Fly through cleansing
And fall into deep rivers

Come inside this
World submerged
Tell me secrets
With your hands

Swim in sanctity
Take your treasure
From the sand
And leave me gasping

Breaking through the
Glass cover
To breathe again
The warm salt air

Treasure

Treasure chest
Hidden
Buried secrets

Crystal jewels
Glitter
Smiling coyly

Iron padlock
Solid
Forced free

You look
You touch
Then awaken

Sweaty palms
Aching dream
Empty bed

Gifts
Sparkle sweetly
Out of reach

Taunting diamonds
Shining darkly
Under cover

Hidden treasure
Search
And find nothing

Join

Wait
Hold my
Hand and
Offer me
Peace
Calmness
Flowing from your
Eyes
And into my
Soul

Can we
Dance now?
Flowing motions
Release and
Holding
Meeting each
Other
Finding our
Steps

Togetherness
Thought it was the
Enemy
But now I
See
We are to
Join
Fingers interlaced
And hearts
Forged into
One

Sandpaper

Raw
Sandpaper
Rubs me
And I fight the
Collision
That happens in
This second

But you are
Over me
Drowning me
In your
Control
And it is
Bliss

Bandages
Hold me
Together
Or I will
Fall apart
In the
Shadow of
Who you are

I get you
And you get me
And it is
Broken glass
That will never
Be put
Together again

Forget

Will you forget me one day
Tempted by the world's candy
Led away by the blonde piper
With her inviting curves
Taken hostage by the
One with sweet charms

Will you forget me one day
Forget the look that
Fed my empty soul
And taught my heart
To beat again
And want and need
And cry for your strong hands

Will you forget me one day
Forget my smile that
Cheered you in the morning light
Leave me on the roadside
Dust flying behind your
Spinning tires
And not even glance back

Will you forget me one day
And see my face in passing
And register only slight familiarity
In place of the passion
That once controlled you
And made my life whole
Will you forget me

Somber

You are a somber spirit
Burdened with the
Weight of your goodness
And wanting to say what you think
And give in to emotion

Your eyes are truth
You hide from your own vision
And resist trusting the rotting wood
That holds your frame steady
And isn't there at all

Your pen is your weapon
And your savior
Your message in a bottle
Reaches me
And I must look away

You are a somber spirit
Finding freedom
And climbing toward forgiveness
And sending a smile to my heart
On your way to other places

5 {Recovery}

~

I will
One day find
Beauty
In my
Disaster

~

Doorway

I have
Stood too long
In the
Doorway
Planning my
Escape or
Entrance
Wheels turning
Thoughts churning
Contemplating a
Painful past and
Hazy future

Futility
I have made a
Mess
Splattered the
Milk
On the
Pristine floor
Then ground
It in with
Muddy boots

Too many
Words
Time for
Silence
My fingernails
Have cut my
Skin from the
Clenching of
Fists
Clinging to my
Will has
Cost me my
Sanity

There is an
Offer on the
Table
Serenity beckons
If I will
Allow my fields
To be
Plowed
If I will just
Surrender

My will wrestles
Itself free
For one last
Plea
Casts the
Fear net
Over my
Eyes
And for a
Moment I
Trust it

God beckons
With no heavy
Sighs or
Force
But with alluring
Quiet
And the
Promise
I will
One day find
Beauty
In my
Disaster

Weight

Bird flies overhead
Free
Navy feathers flickering
In bright sun

I am trapped
With weights tied
To my ankles
And raw wrists

Sweat pours down
My bruised face
As I slowly take
One step at a time

I move cautiously
Over rocky hills
Sharp stones cutting
Bleeding feet

I believe somehow
I could make it
If only I knew
My destination

Child

She is a
Child
Needy
Wanting to
Get her own
Way

Impatient
She forgets
The sun will
Come up
After this
Long night

She clings to
Phantoms
Willing them to
Fill her
Emptiness

Her crutches
Only serve to
Cripple her
Further
And send her
Falling to the
Ground

She must get
Back up
Learn how to
Stand again
Alone
It's time to
Grow up

Peace

Peace
You elude me
Scattered in your far corners
And hidden in the shadows
Of life gone wrong
Plans laid on quicksand
And hearts thrown into the wind
Hurricanes destroy
And I am left
Sobbing in the sand
That was my destiny

Is there a future?
Some distant echo of
A lighthouse
Calling to my wounded soul
Stand up, stand straight
And catch the wings of calm
Ride them softly, gently
Into the setting sun
Find what you now
Hold in your hand
The harmony you call love
The haven you call home

Crayon

Life is
Messy
And I
Seem to
Take my
Crayon and
Scribble
Blotting out any
Good
I'm quite
Skilled
At that

But this
Girl is
Taking
Baby steps
Recognition
Changing the
Mind
Thought by
Thought

Hope
It will
Change
I will
Change
No more
Clinging and
Grasping
Rather
Letting go

Finding
Solace and
Serenity
Surprised that
Faith
Emerges from the
Seed
That is
Surrender

Lessons

Cellar door slams
Feelings bleed from the
Gash of loneliness
Hollow aching moves
Through the air
Cruelty laughs at
Desperate pleas
And I am here
Alone

Left beauty behind
Freedom had me
Trapped in trust
Wanting nothing but
The baby's smile
My arm led by
Strong hands
And I ran from
Love

Chalk on concrete walls
I write my story
To deaf caretakers
Lessons in life
Taught by a failure
Begging to touch
One searching soul
And bring to this
Empty heart
Meaning

Trapped

Trapped
Held back
Curled up
Gasping for thin
Air
Covered in
Fear and
Hurling blame
Cowering
Behind a
Wall
Of my own
Making

I mixed the
Mortar
Trowel in
Hand
Carefully placed
Brick by brick
Locked myself
Inside with
Silence
Fortified by
Numbing
Disguised as
Escape

I'm sure
I screamed
Freedom
Nearly
Ripped my
Throat out
With the
Force
But now I
Wonder
Was it
Just a
Whisper?

So I beg
Them
With my
Eyes
Please see me
Offer help or
I will
Die here
Heart still
Beating but
Soul
Desolate
Buried

I must
Wield the
Sledgehammer
Level self
Take the
Hand that
Reaches to
Lift me
Out and
Finally
Walk the
Steps to
Wholeness

Distance

Words
Eyes and doors
Closing
Done
Self-preservation
Protection
And I am
Lonely

Unaccustomed
To this
Feeling
Shaping my
Thoughts
Alone is
Comforting
But not
This

All the while
Strength is
Returning
Clarity
Maybe that's
Why the
Pain follows
I've ended the
Numbing

Nothing left but
To experience
Fully
The hurt and
Joy and
Struggle
Live in
This moment
Stretch it
Out

Here
I am
Empty and
Filled to
Overflowing
Tightrope walking
Between
Tears and
Peaceful surrender
Finally
Alive

Trust becomes the
Foundation
For learning
Once again
How to
Love

Fog

White blur
Focus
Struggle to make sense of
The How and Why
Fight to see
One strong figure
Outlined in the haze
One open palm
Reaching toward you
One calm voice
Calling the black light
Squint and try and
Search for the answer
And if you see nothing
In the white fog
Turn your eyes inside
And call to yourself
For the Truth that
Makes its way
Into your soul

Comfort

Dust on ivory keys
Whispers of a melody
Somehow locked

Slick white pages
Phrases unwritten
Somewhere hidden

And I sit on the floor
Hoping for the courage
To open myself

I know the flood of feeling
Born from a single note
Hammer hitting strings

I know the gentle release
Arising from a single word
Ink flowing on paper

It's enough for me
To play a melody
No one can hear
In my darkened room

It's enough for me
To reach for a pen
And let the words flow
When the pain is too much

I'll stroke those keys
And let my music free
I'll capture stirring images
And set my soul free
And in this simple creation
I'll find my comfort

Broken

Broken
We are
Behind the
Façade
Under our
Skin

Moments of
Clarity and
Purpose
Find us
Hidden

We hang on
Tightly
Not knowing
They aren't the
Prize

Rather the
Aching
Makes us most
Alive and
Real

So let's
Surrender
To the
Strength
Masquerading as
Weakness

Ladder

Here she
Stands
Feet on solid
Ground
Eyes
Uplifted
Arms strong
Carrying
What is
Needed

It wasn't
Always this
Way
Walls once
Closed in
Held her
Back from
All she was
Meant to
Become

In her
Despair
She began the
Climb
Only to
Find the
Rungs on this
Ladder
Contained loving
Hands

Together they
Ascended
Though there were
Slips and
Skips and
Missteps on these
Stairs
There was
Certain
Triumph

She has
Grown
And now
Offers her
Own hands
Own heart
Own wisdom
To join with
Others in this
Beautiful
Journey

6 {Connection}

~

Where I go from
Here is
Unclear
But this I
Know
When I do
Stand
I will not be
Alone

~

Protected

Protected
Suspended in comfort
From my crying days
Swaddled in pink cotton
Held close to her heartbeat

Protected
His arms of solace
Scratchy chin rubbing
Soft cheeks
Covered in love

Protected
The mother to the man
Always guiding my path
Never to venture
On my own steps
Never to trust
The power in these
Fragile arms
Never to know
The joy of skinned knees
Earned by falling down
Unprotected

Wounded

I have wounded
You
Inflicted the greatest
Pain
On my greatest
Loves
The injury will
Scab
But never heal
Completely

Like a mother
Bird who
Forces her babies
From the
Nest
Far too soon
Because she
Herself must
Fly
I've caused you
Hurt
To save
Myself

There are no
Excuses
Only reasons too
Complex to
Explain
My life is my
Own
You cannot
Look through this
Lens
Nor travel this
Path

My only
Hope is
That you will
One day
See
What it is to be
Healthy and
Happy and truly
Free

That you will
Recognize
This light in my
Eyes
The gift of
Living my
Truth
Trusting my
Heart

That you will
Come to
Me
When your road gets
Rocky
And believe that
I will have
Something
Meaningful and
Beautiful to
Offer

You will
Find me
Waiting

Scales

Metal plates
Hang by
Chains
Shifting slightly
Adjusting to their
Weight
Balance

I can't go
Back
Even if
All the
Reasons
Pile like
Coins and
Pull one side
Down

Talk me
Into it
Logic or
Family or
God
Someone
Make it
Make sense

The faces of my
Children
Eyes dark
Brown
Pierce me with
Their depth
And almost
Tip the
Scales

My reason
Has no place
Here
I must hold
Earth in my
Hands
Rather than
Walk it
Down some
Unknown
Path

Wait in
Silence
For the
Undoing of
Me
So God can
Knit me
Together
Anew

And where
I go from
Here is
Unclear
But this I
Know
When I do
Stand
I will not be
Alone

Sisters

Flash of
Memory
And you are
There
Sister
Hands on my
Back
Pushing me
Higher and
Farther as I
Swing to the
Sky

Chains of
Daisies
Porcelain-tubbed
Bubble baths
And delicate
Dolls
We played and
Shared and
Sang
Together
Companions

Did I ever
Mention
You were my
Foundation
Solid and
Loving and
True
You knew my
Heart
Better than
Anyone
Showered me with
Love

Sometimes I
Miss those
Days and
Girlish giggles
We've grown
Up
But not
Apart
Miles are
Meaningless
A thread –
Stronger and longer –
Binds us

Moss-covered
Paths
Under our
Feet
Have led us
Differently
Life has dealt
Pain and
Loss and
Hope
Yet we are
Tethered
Across our
Journeys

I wish we
Had more
Time
That our
Encounters were
Routine
But we
Have this
Splendid
Day
Filled with
Fun and
Laughter and
Deep
Discussions

Nothing taken for
Granted
My heart
Holds on to
Yours
My mind
Cherishes precious
Thoughts
Of yesterday and
Tomorrow and
Now
And my
Soul
Overflows with
Love
As we are
Bound
Anew

Roots

Solid ground
Smooth stone
And I stand
Sure-footed
Supported by
Who I am
And I know
Her
Now

But what if
He comes
Different and
Challenging and
Strong
What if I
Weaken

Hard rock
Melting into
Quicksand
Swallowing the
Me
I thought I
Knew

Will even this
Face
Be revealed
As a
Façade
Covering the
Hole
Where my
Soul should
Be

Help me
Trust
That I will not
Shrink
That if my
Foundation
Crumbles and
Leaves me
On the
Ground
I will
Stand and
Learn and
Grow
Roots

Maypole

Maypole
Stands tall
In the
Welcoming
Warmth of the
Sun
Ribbons extend
To our outstretched
Hands
And we
Begin to
Move

Our bare
Feet
Flutter lightly
Over soft
Earth
The music is
Alive
Within us
And we are
Free

This dance
Is our
Prayer
Lifts and
Sways and
Moves us
As our
Arms and
Hearts
Almost touch the
Sky

Our faces are
Flushed
From the
Laughter and
Summer
Heat
Our bodies
Joined to the
Source
And to each
Other

As the
Sun sets
We slow and
Rest
Our spirits
Smile
At the
Communion
Of our
True
Selves

Our souls now
Nourished
We leave this
Place
Not empty-
Handed
But with the
Cherished
Memory
Of this glorious
Day we
Danced

End

The last page
This book of my rambling words
Will end
My hidden gift
Shielded from the eyes of strangers
And loved ones
Who would not understand
And cannot tell
Fact from fiction

Someday it will be opened
By someone who knew me
And misses me on rainy nights
And the words may make sense
And the soul may bond with mine
In some familiar destiny
Though we are apart

I close this book
And end this cycle of my life
Keeping my youth intact
While receiving a little of the
Bitter herbs that have
Crept into my life
And grown me up a little

I will begin a new book
And see where it takes me
And who will join me on my journey
Of pen and paper explorations

About the Author

Suzanne Searcy Johnson is a poet who occasionally writes fiction, essays, or whatever comes to mind. She is immensely grateful for family, friends, her dog and cat, and the opportunity to do the work she loves.

~

Also by Suzanne Searcy Johnson
Forty Lives
Available on Amazon

suzannesjohnson.com